# I Have A Confession To Make....

An admission that my curiosity about love and life led me through pain, yet instead of recoiling, I chose to delve deeper. Maybe I'm a masochist.

Elliana Bonilla

BookLeaf Publishing

India | USA | UK

Made with ❤ on the BookLeaf Publishing Platform
www.bookleafpub.in
www.bookleafpub.com

# Dedication

To my village, those who have held me, stayed with me, taught me, healed me. I wouldn't be me without you.

To my husband, I am not me without you. You are my atlas. Thank you for this gift of life that we share.

# Preface

For as long as I can remember I've been told that I'm poetic and/or wise. I'm not a therapist. I'm just an observant empath with a bleeding heart and a self-involved obsession with the Art of seeking home when you don't know where you belong. I hope this collection finds someone who is also struggling with these themes and helps them.

I have spent so much of myself loving others, pleasing others, abiding by their rules; Vultures, willing to take, and feast on my flesh until I'm threadbare.


So, I stopped.

I stopped sharing the moments I love with them.

I stopped giving them access to my most real, beautiful and intimate moments.

I stopped allowing them to see my world.

I started writing these moments down. Remembrance.

These moments are mine.

& now they're yours, too.

-EB

# Acknowledgements

Poetry isn't just someone expelling their emotions into words. it's a combination of words that are sewn together meticulously to evoke emotion, understanding, acceptance. Our words are the most *poetic* way to connect with other.

To all of the poets that I adore, traditional and non-traditional: thank you.

# 1. 333

I've often fallen to my knees in tears over the injustice
that we're forced to live with.
Helpless and alone.
The cacophony of my internal screaming, echoing in my
head, until I'm dazed.

I thought I was born heartbroken, because I hadn't felt
happiness until I was an adult.
Then, one day my mother told me that I was born with a
hole in my heart.
Suddenly, everything clicked.
Can you imagine how much harder I have to work to
love someone?
Despite this, I was always eager to love with an open
heart.

Platonic and romantic heartbreak alike have shattered
me
and each time, I pick the pieces up and put myself back
together.
All the while, the hurt had bought prime real estate in
the hole in my heart.

So, I decided to write.

As a way of releasing the hurt and pain into the universe,
ensuring I am no longer a bunker for the pain of others.

# 2. justice

Is injustice the adversary to apathy?

Do we need this to be the fire that fuels us?

Is the longing for justice a theme?

Do we ever get it?

# 3. The Man Who Sold The World

My mother had intended,
To name me Elliana
The qualm was her husband,
Whose best English, came from Nirvana
I'm grateful for the name they inadvertently selected.
Because it feels fitting, when I feel outcast and rejected

When I was a little girl,
My father was my entire world.
I'd wait up late at night,
Just to hear him arrive.
I felt so lonely when he was away,
So, by myself, I would play.

I'd always felt alone at home
My mom and brother had a language of their own.
I was always trying to relate
But that seemed to earn me more hate.
I'd wait until my dad got back,
To tell him all the ways that I was attacked.
He'd tell me some euphemism
That only barely made me feel less imprisoned.
That when some scars heal, they can be painted gold

And I'd understand them when I got old.

And I'd study him all the time when he was around
Because he was my favorite person as of now
When he got home, he'd watch futbol
"FUCK BENFICA" from the living room, he'd call.
He'd share movies and music that I couldn't
comprehend,
But I'd learn and laugh along, with my dearest bestest
friend.

When I got older and started to date,
It led me to my first heartbreak.
He told me of his first love,
And shared that he understood
That love can drive anyone to madness
and leave behind both joy and sadness.

As time passed by,
I thought he was the coolest guy
Until I turned 24,
He broke my heart worse than before.
It's still a struggle to let it out,
Because forgiveness remains a path in doubt.

We didn't talk for several years,
So I began to collect all my tears.

I placed them in a mason jar
Each drop a story, each drop a scar.
And when it was filled to the brim,
I decided to give the jar to him.
To show him that it still accounts
For every scar and every doubt.

I've tried to create the space,
To allow him in my life someway.
But my heart doesn't trust him
Each word he speaks is paper thin.

Do fathers know the wounds they leave,
or the weight of love their children grieve?
I hope one day to let it go,
To feel the peace I've yet to know.

But until then,
I've learned one thing,
that this journey is just beginning
forgiveness isn't linear,
it's a promise to try and endure
the pain that comes along
when you know hope to belong

# 4. truth

Is knowing the truth our only justice?

Who is it serving?

Who is it hurting?

Do we really need it?

I don't think I want to know.

# 5. Gently Veiled Moments

To have shared moments so gentle, so raw, so real,
You taught me what it meant to be loved,
You showed me what it was like to be seen.

I became addicted to the feeling,
The laughs, the way you lit up when I entered the room.

I never got to say thank you,
For teaching me how to live, how to love, how to feel
Before you, I was a blank slate, tabula rasa.
A canvas untouched, waiting for colors.

You've given me more than I could ever truly thank you
for.
You were my savior,
And I needed you to be.
I didn't know how to be
With you. Without you.

I've wanted to say that I'm sorry.
Sorry for not understanding,
For not loving you the way you deserved.
Sorry for projecting my insecurities so vividly, loudly
Like you were the silk screen to display my traumas.

You didn't deserve that.

We were just kids,

# 6. Trapped Inside Your Heart-Shaped Box

I know this is good for me, I know it's healthy.
But, I can't stop thinking that my growth is stunted.

After everything that I've witnessed and endured,
I want to feel safe.
And, with you, I do.

But why then, do I sometimes crave chaos?
Sometimes I feel resentment because if I want to love
you
& I do,
that means I agree to stay within the confines of your
world.

But, your world is peaceful.
Your world is gentle.
Your world is kind of boring.
Your world doesn't have implicit lies, family secrets,
trauma bonds.

And, I want to be safe and happy.
I'm happy with you, but my mind doesn't wander.

I don't drift into creative spaces as freely.
You're pragmatic in a way that's important.
But, it doesn't leave room for mystery, mischief,
adventure.

I didn't know that safety meant walls would be risen so
that I can't flee,
at the first argument.
If I did, perhaps I'd have given up the pursuit for it long
ago.
I've always preferred demolition in order to create
Because after all, you can't build on blighted terrain

You're safe and I'm happy that I am now too.
Even if that means sometimes I can't see the outside,
and I feel the wind from the lid closing rapidly above me.

# 7. "What'll Teach Me"

When you're growing up,
something they don't tell you
is that losing friends, hurts too.

No one extrapolates
on how to avoid those mistakes.
Since I promised a confession,
I hope you learn from this lesson:

I wanted to feel alive, desired
so it was my best friend's boyfriend, that i admired.

I told her she should get over him,
and later at night, i'd end up under him.
I called her c r a z y, told her she was obsessed
as i stared in the mirror puffing out my chest.
this friendship was one of convenience,
and it inevitably passed, like the seasons.

Next, i found a friend who held darkness,
"she's just like me", I guessed.

She dated my brother and loved him dearly,
I hated that she couldn't see clearly.

He was using her and for that i levy,
she should've never started something so heavy.
On and off, they'd end their affair.
And each time she'd cry,
he'd call me paranoid, terrified.
He had a girlfriend he loved immensely
Because of this he'd beg intensely
He didn't want anyone to know he was cheating on his
love
So, he requested help, from me, his blood.
I accepted, bc after all it was my duty.
To protect him, even if it felt untrue to me.
So i told her to leave him alone and find a new man
I called her c r a z y
assured her that he wouldn't respond, in advance.

Though this friendship was rough for us both,
she taught me something I carry close.
Don't ever speak when you're mad,
because words, can never be taken back.

I acknowledge now that I was toxic.
I hated myself for it, "I'm obnoxious".
Forgiving myself was hard enough.
I recognized all of my bluffs.
And, though I cannot atone for it all,
Please know I've learned from the fall

From self-assuredness to self-doubt
I know now that there is no amount
Of comparing myself to other folks
That will shrink this self-made hoax
Of insecurity, and lovelessness
I'm dedicated to growing from this mess.

If I don't know then I cannot grow and
If I don't feel that I cannot heal.
This mantra makes me radiate,
And practice love instead of hate.

# 8. i still wish you nothing but the best

I hope your hell is the loop you built,
A mirror of every word you spoke for yourself.
You wore presence like a mask,
But your silence was always louder.
I wanted to be seen, understood, and heard.

So I whispered to anyone who'd listen,
Even as red flags danced in my periphery.
I called it connection.

I crafted myself as a savior,
While quietly resenting the weight I carried.
A martyr for a friendship that was never whole,
never equal, only fragments of need
Passed back and forth like a tired currency.
We were both exhausted.

Though my heart bore its own hole
I filled it with guilt and penance,
Hoping it was enough.

But friendship isn't a ledger to balance.
It's not 50/50 or debts repaid.

It's the language of care written in effort,
A thank you whispered without asking.

And I wonder, as I leave you behind,
If you ever understood the weight
Of being a home for someone else's wounds.

# 9. lonelier together

Chronic Loneliness,
A universal aching
Don't we hurt the same?

# 10. the light

In a childhood home where lovelessness reigned,
I was immersed, involuntarily
in a family that didn't know how to show it.
*Value was placed on performance*


How much can a child truly achieve?
So you learn to mimic adults.
You master the art of service,
While your own needs fade into the background
& you forget how to be who you are.


It makes sense, then,
why I sought out partners who professed love
before the weeks turned to months.
I thought I could be their salvation,
Siphoning the small fragments of myself I dared to share,
Pouring them into the depths of their emptiness,
feeding their longing, desire, ego.


Shower me with material items until I dematerialize.
An idea. A concept. Something soft enough to mold.
Not too pretty, not too smart, just enough
to lighten their darkness and fill their voids.

But even shadows cast by passion fade,
and I became adept at playing a part
because that was better than being alone, or abandoned.
Love wasn't sacred. It was a role, a performance,
never a refuge. It was precarious at best.

And now, I crave a love unshaken,
a quiet truth, the stillness of stability.

# 11. Your life has been hard enough, I won't play games

There's no way to explain the connectedness I feel with
you,
Unless we've met in another lifetime.
We've walked similar paths,
Each carrying different lessons.
I wish I had been there to see you then.
The phrase, *"You can't pour from an empty glass,"*
Must have been written for the way you fill my cup.
You ARE the loveliest cup.
We are tethered to one another
In a way I never knew could exist.
I never understood why *home* mattered,
Until I found one with you.
My view of love and marriage
Was shaped by those who couldn't love as we do.
I didn't know love until I met you.
To love you is to admit my vulnerability
The thought of being without you makes me unravel.
Each morning we wake, smiles and laughter entwined.
When I'm away from you,
My heart searches for you everywhere.
When I'm away from you for too long,

Everything begins to look like you, sound like you.
You loved me to life.

# 12. Phoenix

I've always been told that I'm prone to burn out.
But I've always loved the way things disintegrate
After they've burned fiercely
To give all your energy in one last, ephemeral outburst,
To become ashes,
Peacefully returning to the earth.
A quiet reunion, fertile, waiting,
Where roots may drink deeply and find new life.
It's beautiful, really,
That you can tell I'm giving all of myself to this.
As ashes, I'll scatter beneath the weight of the world,
Sink into the soil, feed the seeds of tomorrow,
And rise again.
To ignite,
To burn,
To rise and fall the way that fire demands.

# 13. maladaptive servitude

My brother won't share his PlayStation controller,
We argue, name-calling, getting bolder.
You threaten to leave whenever we fight,
So, I panic a little when it becomes night.
I don't want you to go,
Because without you, I know,
I'd be cast away and left alone.
I start to recoil and my anger wavers,
I start to submit, doing whatever it favors.
You never leave, but as I grow old,
I believe servitude is my love language,
Doing whatever it takes to avoid the same damage.
I'll give myself away, hoping I'm sufficient,
Searching for clues that their love is consistent.
Never daring to ask for the same in return,
But can you blame me? It's what I learned.

# 14. David by Michelangelo

We've always loved laying in the grass together.
There's something sacred about the earth beneath us.
Our bodies merging with the world's pulse
the wind crashing into the leaves,
a symphony of nature's quiet urgency

A wild surrender
Unspoken, instinctual
relentless, gentle, tender

The blades of grass caressing our skin,
imitating your fingers trailing up my spine.
In it's embrace, you're both the soil and the sky,
The sun and the moon,
The roots and the bloom
The pushing and the pulling of gravity's strongest force
The electricity, calmness, surrender, desire, connection
that runs through my body, has never existed inside me
simultaneously.

like the grass beneath us,
it's not tame,
not always neat or controlled,

but in its chaos,
there's a freedom

# 15. all living things

I found a mouse trap in a crevice
of my mom's kitchen cabinet.
The mouse, small and trembling,
met its end between metal and wood.
I witnessed his struggle,
his last attempts to survive.
I stayed up all night and I cried.
Years later, at my in-law's house,
I saw another this time in a sticky trap.
Frantic and begging. My heart screamed mercy.
Together, we freed him,
donning gloves to avoid a bite,
setting him gently into the night.
Since then, I've harmed nothing.
Spiders are captured and liberated,
never crushed.
Even my fears have grown tender.
Love is contagious.
Through small acts,
we teach the world to be softer.

# 16. trauma bonds

Have you ever wondered
Why everything you touch begins to crumble?
Parents are meant to create safety,
Spaces for growth, curiosity, learning.
You never did.
You ostracized me,
Made me hate the skin I was in
The way I spoke and thought.
But I grew up.
I chose not to participate anymore.
You grew angry,
Until your hatred erupted,
Spilling decades of poison
Onto the "family" you built.
We are products of the love we never received.
And yet, the little girl you broke
Learned to trust.
She learned to love.
She learned that being cast aside
Was the universe's quiet way
Of guiding her to a safer place.

# 17. fading roots

My anger has faded,
Though its embers still glow faintly.

I can't blame you.
We were told to love,
We weren't shown.

Love was taught in fragments.
Fierce, aggressive, angry,
intense and hardened.
"Family first," they said,
While living miles from their own.

How could we learn,
When even their roots were torn?
I can't be mad at you,
When I was there too

Soft clay, still kneaded,
While you dried in isolation.
Bone-dry, leather-hard,
Hardened by hands that never returned.

That anyone tried to understand me.

feels like a miracle.

I softened, so we're not the same anymore,
and for that I'm sorry.

# 18. Returning Home

I crave being gentle.
I crave being softer in how I represent what matters to
me
and how I present who I am to those around me.
There is always a disconnect that occurs,
A fire in my chest
My heart racing when I hear something triggering.
A need to defend, to protect.

My husband shows me that I don't need to default to
anger.
I can be understood when I'm sad.
I don't need to scream, I can be heard when I speak.
I don't need to express myself in ways that are
outrageous to be seen,
He shows me how to come back home to myself,
with love, always.

# 19. "history repeats itself & that's just how it goes"

I never liked history class
endlessly studying the supremacy
of indistinguishable old white men.

My mind would wander:
"Why does it matter what happened back then?
What about what's happening now?"

I didn't see it then,
how much this reflected who I was,
how unaware I truly was.

But now I know
We cannot truly honor our victories or understand our
failures,
without the wisdom that reflection brings.
Reflection on our past, our experiences.
Without reflection, growth remains impossible,
and without growth, we are lost in the face of adversity.

# 20. love owes no debts

As a child, I had a plan,
an idea of who I'd become.
When I grew older, I could see it clearly
a path laid out in pragmatic steps.

I'd graduate at 21,
work hard to make $80,000 a year,
and start budgeting
to pay my parents back.

I'd give them a lump-sum check—
my way of saying,
"Thank you for all of your sacrifices. It was worth it."

But how do you repay a lifetime of love
with numbers, and the weight of a checkbook?
I'm still calculating the cost
of a childhood that feels both given and owed.

# 21. the recipe to happiness

In this brief time on earth,
we live several lives,
each one unfolding in its turn.

Be present for them all,
love deeply, feel fully,
chase your passions,
and care for those who matter.

Stay true to yourself,
authentic in every form

the world will catch up
and understand in time
you'll give it no choice.